Written by Catherine Zoller
Pictures by Mr. Sketches

RHYME & REASON
R&R
SERIES

"GETTING THESE BOOKS IN PEOPLE'S HANDS SO PEOPLE'S HANDS PICK UP THE BOOK."

ABOUT THE AUTHOR

Catherine Zoller is a writer from Tulsa, Oklahoma,
With a husband, three kids and half a college diploma.

Many years ago the Lord spoke to her one night
And said simply and clearly, "I want you to write."

So she jumped out of bed and grabbed paper and pen
And waited on the sofa for Him to speak to her again.

At last came the dawn with the dew and the mist,
But all she had written was half a grocery list.

Still she never forgot the words spoken that night;
All she had to learn was that His timing's always right.

Now she's written some rhymes that tell the Bible story
From Genesis to Revelation and reveal God's glory.

The hope in her heart is to show everyone
That reading God's word can be lots of fun.

It will instruct you and teach you and change your heart,
And this little book is designed to help you start!

Genesis: The Rhyme and Reason Series by Catherine Zoller
Copyright ©2009 by Catherine Zoller
Printed in the USA

ISBN 978-1-58169-337-9
For worldwide distribution

Rhyme & Reason Ministries International • P.O. Box 470994 • Tulsa, OK 74147-0994
You can learn more about Catherine Zoller at www.catherinezoller.com

ABOUT THE ILLUSTRATOR

Artist Mr. Sketches is also known by some
As Mr. David Wilson, and he thinks art is fun.

The nickname Mr. Sketches came from a T.V. show
That TBN broadcast for three years in a row.

His lovely wife, Karen, likes to teach the first grade;
They moved around a bit, but when they got to Tulsa stayed.

Art from the heart helps God's kids succeed
So as David sketches, this is his creed:

"Whatever Reason or Rhyme, whatever season or time,
With a broad point or with fine, it's time to draw the line!"

DEDICATION

This book is dedicated to the Lord God above
Who rescued and saved me and washed me with His love.

All I have and all I am, I freely give to Him,
'Cause He has set me free from the bondage of sin.

I offer these books to be used for His glory
And pray they will help tell the world His story.

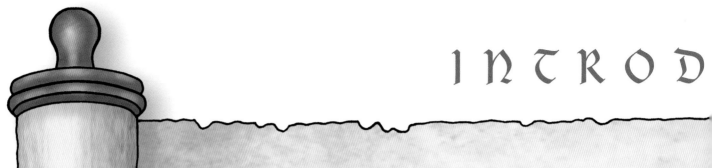

Come gather 'round me children and incline to me your ear
Because there's something important I want you all to hear.

I wrote this little book, you see, especially for you,
To help you understand the things that God is tryin' to do.

It's a book about creation and the story goes on from there
To reveal our Father's loving heart to people everywhere.

The Bible is God's love letter He's written just for us,
Containing hidden treasures to discover and discuss.

The hope within my heart today is that you'll clearly see
The bounty of God's goodness that's in store for you and me.

Too many people think that God is just a mean old man
Who waits to bop us on the head or slap us on the hand.

They think that He looks mainly for the things that we've done wrong,
Then somehow they lose focus of His purpose all along.

This purpose is to enter a relationship with Him;
To walk with Him in victory and freedom from all sin.

Because the God of heaven who made everything we see
Wants more than anything to be a friend to you and me.

He wants to draw us close to Him and lead us hand in hand
To help us face the trials of life and love our fellow man.

It's always been His goal for us, and never has it changed,
Especially since the Fall from grace when man became estranged.

So read the poem I've written on the following few pages,
And let it teach you something new about the Rock of Ages.

Look for all the places where our God reveals His heart,
See His hand of mercy that He offered from the start.

So let your heart be open to the things He plans to do,
Then simply pray and ask Him to reveal Himself to you.

And ask God now to show you what He's planning for your life,
Which is to live in harmony and not in sin and strife.

So come on, laugh a little bit, and let's all have some fun
As you read this rhyming story of the true things God has done!

This is the one true story
of how everything began.
Because of love our God began
to formulate a plan.

For six short days He labored as He shouted His commands,
Up popped the stars, the trees, the seas, the mountains and the lands.

Then God released the power of His vast imagination,
Creating all the animals and all the vegetation.

He made cobras, camels, bison, and leopards with their spots,
Ostriches and hummingbirds, and fish with stripes and dots.

Butterflies and fireflies, mosquitoes, spiders, gnats,
Chipmunks, turtles, rabbits, and all kinds of dogs and cats.

He thought of oranges, kiwis, pears, and lovely red cranberries,
Guavas, melons, apricots, bananas and red cherries.

He made some bitter, made some sour,
made others to be sweet;
He fashioned all the vegetables
our mothers make us eat.

Like Brussels sprouts, potatoes, and the funny, odd kumquat,
And somehow out of nothing He created quite a lot!

Genesis 1:1-25

7

Now don't think He was finished with all the great things He'd done,
'Cause next He made the people, and the fun had just begun.

He longed for special fellowship to share His perfect love,
To walk with folks and to talk with them like fellowship above.

God said, "Let Us make man in Our image and Our likeness,
Living beings who reflect our friendship and our rightness."

At first He made a man but saw he was without a wife.
He took a rib from Adam's side and then brought Eve to life.

He settled them in Eden where they found amazing stuff,
Then gave them just one simple rule so life would not be tough.

They could not eat the fruit off of the Garden's center tree,
But in every other action they were completely free.

They had all that they needed, even God to be their friend.
Everything was perfect; it would never need to end.

Genesis 1:26-2:25

8

9

But soon there came the serpent
   who was crafty and so sly
And told Eve if she ate the fruit
   she wouldn't *really* die.

She reached her hand out for the fruit
   and took a great big bite,
Then offered some to Adam
   when he came into her sight.

The serpent had deceived her to
   think she'd be wise like God.
They broke the flow of fellowship
   and now they stood sin-flawed.

And at that very instant
   both their eyes were opened wide.
Instead of fellowship with God,
   there was a great divide.

Genesis 3:1-7

11

They hid themselves behind a bush and fashioned clothes from leaves,
For they had disobeyed and knew that God would not be pleased.

Foolish children! The sovereign God knew just what they'd done.
It made Him sad to think that they would try to hide and run.

After spending time with Him in sweet communication,
Now their disobedience would cause great desolation.

Genesis 3:7-20

They had to leave the Garden and close fellowship with Him,
So God Himself made clothes for them from animal's soft skin.

Yet in this time of crisis, our God promised He'd begin
To implement a plan to bring fallen folks back to Him.

Years later, through the line of Eve, would come the Chosen One,
Who'd crush the serpent's head and be God's one and only Son.

Genesis 3:21-24

13

But first we find the outcasts
had been blessed with strapping sons,
Then one had killed the other
before they had heard of guns.

It seems that Abel's sacrifice
was pleasing from the start,
While his brother's offering
came from a selfish heart.

So Cain lashed out in anger
and he struck his brother dead.
Yet God marked him for safety's sake
and so away he fled.

The grave sin of the father
had now spread down to the son.
And Man's corrupted nature
is a curse for everyone.

Genesis 4:1-15

14

 **S**oon thereafter Adam split,
     because he was now dead,
And Noah checked in next in line
     and this is what God said:

"Now listen very carefully
     to all you need to do.
Please load up all the animals
     in your own floating zoo.

"The world is full of sin
     and it is causing Me great pain,
So for the first time ever
     I will wash it clean with rain.

"No one on earth has listened to
     My urgent pleas to turn
Away from sinful, selfish ways
     and come to Me to learn.

"But you, My faithful servant,
     have found favor in My sight
Because you have looked unto Me
     and desired to do right."

By faith ol' brother Noah
     believed all the words he heard,
And dared within his heart to take
     the great God at His word.

Genesis 6:1-18

For one hundred twenty years
Noah worked on that huge boat.
At last came the awaited day
when it was time to float.

He loaded up the animals
he'd counted two by two,
Then checked each pair off of his list
as they went walking through.

Genesis 6:19-22

He grabbed two swinging chimpanzees and put them in their bunks,
Then herded up two elephants and had them pack their trunks.

He brought aboard two graceful swans and peacocks with their plumes.
He loaded up some shovels and he brought aboard some brooms.

On board were aardvarks and zebras and all that's in between.
The noise and pandemonium created quite a scene.

He fastened all their stalls and stacked up food for the long trip,
Then took one last look 'round at all the cargo on his ship.

He called together his three sons who brought along their wives.
These were the only ones on earth to escape with their lives.

Then God, Himself, He closed the door and shut them in their boat.
All eight of them got settled in to wait to finally float.

All of the neighbors who had laughed with mockery and disdain
Were shocked when at long last it really *did* begin to rain.

For forty days and nights torrents of rain came crashing down.
All those who'd scoffed when Noah preached were swept away and drowned.

Genesis 7:1-24

After many days and nights the ark perched upon a hill,
And some folks, to this very day, say that it's up there still.

Frozen on Mount Ararat as lasting testimony;
The flood really happened--it's not legend or baloney.

For God desired that Noah and his kin make a fresh start,
And sent a shining rainbow with a promise from His heart.

God made a solemn covenant with Noah His true son.
He said, "I'll never make another flood like this one come!"

When all the floods receded and the land began to dry,
They all stepped off the boat and then began to multiply.

Genesis 8:1-9:17

19

 ow kids, I hate to tell you
    that it didn't take too long
Before they started practicing
    the things they knew were wrong.

They built a massive tower and thought heaven they could reach,
But God, He interrupted them, and muddled all their speech.

They gestured like Italians
    and no one could understand
All the different languages
    now spoken in their land.

They shouted out in Russian,
    in Swahili, and in Greek,
And when they saw the state of things
    knew they were up a creek.

Not one of them could understand what anybody said;
The Lord exposed their pride and left their building project dead.

They had failed to recognize the God above who'd made 'em
And thought that they alone had made a mighty civilization.

In His great compassion God was giving them the creed
That only when we trust in Him will we truly succeed.

Genesis 11:1-9

Soon ol' Noah checked out,
    'cause he was finally dead,
And in checked brother Abram,
    and this is what God said:

"With your wife and servants you must now depart this place
'Cause I'm using just the two of you to start up a new race."

God wanted for Himself a people consecrated;
A "family" He could love who would all be dedicated.

Genesis 12:1-9

God had promised Abram He'd provide him with a son,
But Abram's old wife Sarai said, "Hey! I can get it done!"

So she brought in her maidservant to act as Abram's wife,
And from that moment on there was resentment, shame and strife.

Once again it goes to show that we must trust in Him
To bring about His plans for us, but only He knows when.

Hagar bore Ishmael but God was not yet done.
His plan was for old Sarai to deliver Abram's son.

Genesis 16:1-6

Before all that could come about there was a funeral pyre;
God judged Sodom and Gomorrah with brimstone and with fire.

Because both towns were nasty pits of evil and of sin,
And it was quite impossible to find ten righteous men.

Living there in Sodom was Abram's cousin Lot,
But it was hard to say if old Lot loved God or not.

At the very last moment angels pulled him from the city
'Cause God knew that the fireworks were not going to be pretty.

The angels said to leave, to neither look back nor to halt,
But Lot's wife turned her head to see and she was turned to salt.

Let those cities be a lesson to anyone who sees;
God won't ignore our sin and let us do just as we please.

If they had heeded God's warning and turned away from sin,
God, with His heart of mercy, would have pardoned *all* of them.

For He's a holy God who wants to bring us out of sin
Because He's eager for us all to be holy like Him.

Genesis 19:1-29

God then changed the couple's names to Sarah and Abraham,
Establishing a covenant that forever would stand.

Then finally old Sarah became pregnant with a son,
God had foretold it long ago and now Isaac had come.

So now it's Isaac's turn to arrive in this family scene;
You won't believe what happened next, and here is what I mean:

Genesis 21:1-7

God instructed Abraham to take young Isaac's life;
To lay him on the altar and kill him with his knife.

So faith-filled Abraham obeyed all that God had to say,
'Cause in his heart he knew that God could surely make a way.

Then God spoke up again and said, "Wait! Now I truly see
That even the son promised you, you don't love more than Me."

Genesis 22:1-19

Eventually it's Isaac's turn
to find himself a bride,
So he sent his servant back home
to prospect far and wide.

And so Rebekah came to him to be his lovely bride,
And she was there to comfort him after his mother died.

Rebekah soon was pregnant and she bore her husband twins;
When they grew up into young men, again the fun begins.

Genesis 24:1-67 & 25:19-26

28

God declared the older son would have to serve the younger,
And so it happened just like that because of Esau's hunger.

One day famished Esau decided that a bowl of beans
Was worth the price of his birthright and everything it means.

With the help Rebekah gave and the intent to mislead
Jacob schemed for the birthright to fulfill his selfish need.

They covered up his arms with the fur off a wild beast,
And then he served his father a delicious home-cooked feast.

The old man was deceived because he could not see too well,
So when Esau came home that night, his whole expression fell.

Though Jacob got the blessing, the boy was soon to learn
That each will reap the seeds we sow in life at every turn.

Genesis 25:27-34 & 27:1-41

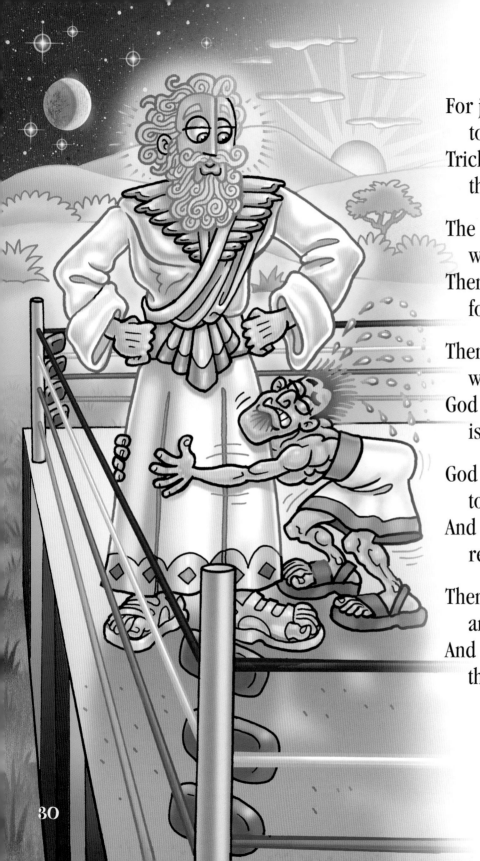

For just as he chose trickery
　　to swindle and deceive,
Tricks determined who would be
　　the *first* wife that he received.

The trickster was then tricked
　　when he took Leah as his bride,
Then worked another seven years
　　for Rachel by his side.

Then Jacob wrestled with the Lord
　　who always will prevail;
God showed him self-reliance
　　is the way to surely fail.

God wanted his son Jacob
　　to rely on Him alone,
And not strive to accomplish
　　reaching God's will on his own.

Then God took Jacob's given name
　　and called him Israel,
And thus began a nation
　　that is known by that name still.

Genesis 29:1-30 & 32:24-28

 e *finally* married Rachel and when all was said and done,
Ol' Jacob wound up numbering one dozen mighty sons.

His favorite son was Joseph, this was plain for all to see,
But it stirred up among the rest a corporate jealousy.

Then Jacob made a special coat and handed it to Joe,
And when the brothers saw the thing, it made their hatred grow.

Genesis 37:1-4

Another problem surfaced soon when young Joe had a dream.
His brothers each resented it and all that it would mean.

Joe saw his dad and older brothers bowing down to him
While he assumed authority o'er every one of them.

They plotted and they planned and they sold Joseph as a slave,
They felt that they were justified in selling Daddy's fave.

Before they sent him off they took his many colored coat,
Convincing Jacob Joe was dead with red blood from a goat.

Genesis 37:5-36

33

They sold him into Egypt
    where as a slave he'd toil,
But to God and his boss Potiphar
    he was always loyal.

Mrs. Potiphar decided
    she was interested in Joe,
But when he wouldn't give in
    she said, "Joe has gotta go!"

And so ol' Joe found he'd been
    treated wrong again,
But by his choices and God's grace
    he was kept out of sin.

His circumstances looked as if
    the good Lord had forgotten,
Because in spite of all He'd pledged,
    Joe's life looked very rotten.

Genesis 39:1-23

34

But God was still at work to bring His mighty plans to pass,
To fulfill all His promises too wonderful to grasp.

Meanwhile, down in the prison, in the cell they kept him in,
Joe met two men with dreams that he interpreted for them.

When everything then happened just like he said it would,
He asked the one whose life was spared, "A favor, if you could?"

Genesis 40:1-23

Then Pharaoh had a dream one night
    that no one could explain,
With seven fat and skinny cows
    and seven heads of grain.

It seems that all the skinny ones
    were eating up the plump,
And the thought of such an image
    had the Pharaoh truly stumped.

He called for all his wise men to interpret the strange dream,
But no one had an inkling as to what it all might mean.

It was then that the cupbearer remembered our friend Joe.
They sent for him at once and brought him up from down below.

Joe explained to Pharaoh that his dream was the real deal,
That the things about to happen were God's plan He'd now reveal.

Said Joseph, "God is telling you the things that He is plannin'--
Seven years of plenty and then seven years of famine.

"Now the wisest thing for you to do is store away some grain
So the people can still eat when the Lord withholds the rain."

Then Pharaoh said to Joseph, "Hey, you're such a clever guy!
Why don't you head this program up so no one has to die?"

Joe was freed right on the spot and made second in command;
And just as he had told the king, a famine struck the land.

36   *Genesis 41:1-57*

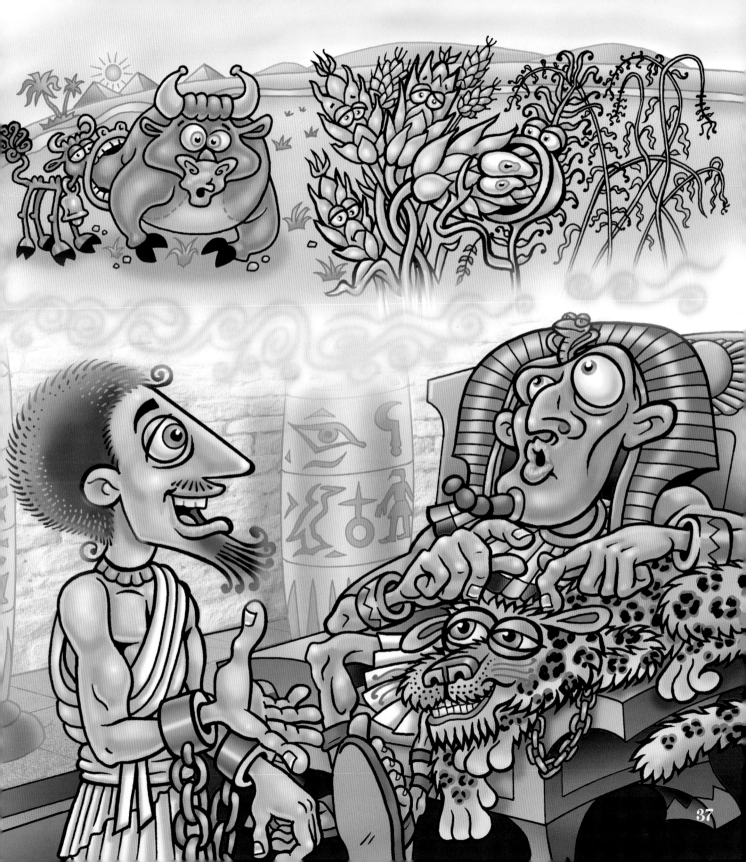

Now Jacob heard that Egypt had some food that they could buy.
He said, "You're going on a trip," and told his sons goodbye.

So the brothers went to Egypt for the food to stay alive,
But along with all the grain came the shock of their whole lives!

For they traveled to the land and bowed down at Joseph's feet
And said, "Oh master, let us buy your excess grain to eat."

Joe recognized his brothers but not one of them knew him,
So he decided he would play a little trick on them.

Genesis 42:1-8

He yelled, "I know you're *spies*
    who've come to Egypt to seek
Secret information showing
    ways our nation's weak!"

The brothers, horrified, exclaimed,
    "No! That we'd never do!
We're just ten hungry brothers,
    with another brother, too."

"Okay," said Joe, "Then listen to
    the things I have to say:
Nine can go, return back home,
    but one of you must stay.

"Bring your youngest brother back
    to Egypt and to me,
And after I have seen him,
    then I'll set your family free."

Genesis 42:9-24

39

Later when they stopped to sleep, each one opened his sack.
Each brother, besides the grain, was given his money back.

They all were frightened by this thing; their thoughts were voiced by one.

He said, "Oh my, dear brothers, what is this that God has done?" *Genesis 42:25-28*

So all nine brothers trudged along to get back to their land,
And had to tell old Jacob things had gotten out of hand.

He was distraught by this bad news but what else could he do?
He sent along young Benjamin with gifts and money too. *Genesis 42:29-43:15*

When they returned to Egypt, Joseph hosted a huge feast,
And seated all his brothers from the oldest to the least.

He had arranged for his servant
to fill all their bags up,
And down inside of Benjamin's,
to hide Joe's silver cup.

The servant willingly obeyed
his master Joe's command
As they loaded up the caravan
to return to their land.

They had not gotten far when
the king's guard rode and caught up,
And searching through the bags
they found in Ben's the silver cup.

Genesis 43:6-44:13

Joe asked, "When shown kindness by me is this how you repay?
To steal my silver cup? Now Ben will surely be my slave!"

Then Judah ran to Joseph with a deep and heavy sigh,
Said, "If father loses Benjamin, then surely he will die.

"We had another brother whom we haven't seen for years,
And even now the thought of Joseph brings our dad to tears.

"If he were now, again, to lose another favorite son,
He simply couldn't take it and he would become undone."

Genesis 44:14-34

Then Joseph couldn't stand it for another minute more.
He cried out, "*I* AM JOSEPH WHOM YOU SOLD OFF YEARS BEFORE!"

His brothers were quite frightened when they saw that it was true,
But Joseph said, "Don't be afraid, I'll do no harm to you."

Genesis 45:1-4

44

So Joe forgave his brothers for the evil in their hearts,
And said God worked it for their good back from the very start.

The mercy and the restoration God desires for all
Was evident in Joseph's life and demonstrates His call.

So Joe ruled over all of them just as his dream had said,
But power and position never swelled to fill his head.

Genesis 45:5-15

45

So Joseph and his father
 were united in the end,
And all the family came to share
 Egyptian land with him.

Now once again it was a clever
 thing for God to do,
Because it kept His people
 separated, faithful, true.

Can't you just imagine
 their tremendous celebration?
To see the hand of God at work
 filled each one with elation.

'Cause His plans are always perfect,
 all His promises are true,
Though we cannot always grasp them
 and don't always have proof.

They knew God had accomplished
 all He said that He would do;
The same He does for all His own--
 including me and you!

Genesis 46:1-34

47

As this big story carries on, the plot becomes quite muddy.
But that's all I can tell you now, 'cause that's another study.